'The Radiant Dawn by Tom Parsons is a gem of a read. While few of us are strangers to Luke chapters one and two, this Advent devotional encourages us to slow down and meditate on what is affectionately called the Christmas Story, but is in truth the historical record of the arrival of the Messiah. Tom manages to help us sweep aside familiarity and replace it with fresh awe and adoration, not only for the Babe in the manger, but also the Christ on the cross. The craziness of the Christmas season is put into perspective as our spiritual preparation is prioritised in these short, challenging readings. Not intended as a cosy read, The Radiant Dawn challenges us to engage once more with the Christ of Christmas.'

Catherine Campbell, Speaker and author of *Broken Works Best* and *Journey with Me*

'This book exists because Tom Parsons loves his wife and loves God's Word about the coming into the world of His Son, the Lord Jesus. And now, we get to enjoy these twenty-five brief but insightful reflections on the opening of Luke's gospel in the run up to Christmas Day. Tom's writing is culturally engaged, personally applied and biblically informed. I'd like to put a copy of The Radiant Dawn into the homes of everyone in our church family before December 1st, and to pass it on to their neighbours and friends who don't know the Lord.'

Craig Dyer, Associate Pastor of Harper Church, Glasgow, and Training Director for Christianity Explored Ministries

'December can be an overwhelming season. How to find the peace and joy that Christmas is meant to be all about? Enter Tom Parsons with a devotional to guide us through 25 days over Christmas. Read. Enjoy. Worship.'

Dr Josh Moody, Senior Pastor, College Chu

'These outstanding little commentaries are a gift to the church. They come out of Tom's love for Christ and his love for his wife, Katie, and I have found them deeply moving.'

Rico Tice, All Souls Church, Langham Place

'Fresh, inspiring, challenging, practical. Tom Parsons makes the opening chapters of Luke's Gospel come alive in these daily bible studies for Advent. Inspiration and encouragement for every day of December as we wait for the coming of the Christ-child.'

John Wyatt, author and paediatrician, London

The Radiant Dawn

25 DAILY BIBLE READINGS
LUKE 1-2 FOR ADVENT

Tom Parsons

10 Publishing
a division of 10 of those.com

Copyright © 2018 by Tom Parsons

First published in Great Britain in 2018
First published by 10Publishing in 2019

The right of Tom Parsons to be identified as the Author of this Work has been asserted by him in accordance with the Copyright, Designs and Patents Act 1988.

British Library Cataloguing in Publication Data
A record for this book is available from the British Library

ISBN: 978-1-912373-91-8

Designed and typeset by Pete Barnsley (CreativeHoot.com)

Printed in the UK

10Publishing, a division of 10ofthose.com
Unit C, Tomlinson Road, Leyland, PR25 2DY, England

Email: info@10ofthose.com
Website: www.10ofthose.com

1 3 5 7 10 8 6 4 2

Introduction

Welcome to the joyful opening chapters of Luke's Gospel. They have always seemed to me to glow, and not only through their association with the Christmas lights that sparkle in the darkness of December. Luke presents Jesus' entry into the world as the radiant dawn of an eternal day. There's music as well as light. Jesus entered this world accompanied by songs of celebration. Since then, I'm sure these two chapters have inspired more music than any other section of the Bible. Glowing with light and ringing with music, Luke's nativity account invites us to experience the joy Jesus' birth still gives.

I've noticed that committed Christians often find December more exhausting than others, not less. Perhaps that's inevitable. The pre-Christmas build up is busy enough in the family and at work. In addition, we want to seize the many opportunities open to us for sharing and celebrating the Christmas message with others. I will be very happy if these daily notes can enable a busy Christian to experience Jesus' joy inwardly while serving him outwardly.

I have assumed that readers are already committed followers of Jesus. However, I'd like to give a word of encouragement to others. You may know for sure that you don't yet belong to Jesus. Or you might be unsure whether you do or not – perhaps never having realised that each one of us needs to make a personal response to him. I hope that you will read on. As you discover more fully what these familiar Bible passages mean, I pray that you will believe the good news and receive Jesus' light and joy.

It is important to read the relevant passage from Luke before looking at the notes each day. Sometimes the same passage is repeated several times. It is intended that you revisit those passages in full every day, rather than skipping them and going straight to the notes. The prayers are written in the "we" / "us" form. I hope you will feel free to change that to "I" / "me" if you find that more helpful.

I first wrote these notes for Katie, my wife, in December 2017 after she discovered she had no Advent reading material at hand. Each daily reading appeared in the appropriate numbered bags that hang on our tree-shaped Advent calendar. Katie's clear and settled faith is of exactly the sort Luke wanted to instil in his dedicatee, Theophilus. I dedicate this short book to her.

O Radiant Dawn,

Splendour of eternal Light,

Sun of Justice:

come, shine on those who dwell in

darkness and the shadow of death.

Antiphon for 21st December

Everyone expects a toddler to be wobbly on their feet, but if they still wobble in the same way as a teenager, there's a problem!

The same principle is true in the Christian life. It's no wonder new believers sometimes wobble. The problem is that too many of us remain stuck in the half-light of our early impressions of Jesus. We go on wobbling for years.

Luke wrote his account of Jesus' life to give a new believer – Theophilus – stability in his faith. It's true, "stability" doesn't sound very exciting. But actually, there is no greater treasure than a settled and clear certainty about Jesus and his Kingdom.

How did Luke intend to give Theophilus this stability? It's vital we all know the answer, because God uses the same strategy today.

First, Luke intended to give an accurate account of the events. There's no stability if we're not certain that the events of Jesus' life – his birth, death and resurrection – really happened. Luke had conducted careful research, going back to the earliest eye-witnesses. As we read his account, we can be confident that we have the facts.

Second, he intended to give a full understanding of these events and their significance. In verse 1, Luke hints that their meaning had been explained long before they took place: Jesus *fulfilled* God's promises to Israel. Luke will show how that happened in his own "orderly account" (verse 3), orderly not just because he writes the events down in the right order, but because they make sense in the light of all God's promises.

There is no time in the year when it's easier to get off balance than in the manic pre-Christmas build up. We tend to shop, party and worry like everyone else. It's possible to fall flat on our faces – spiritually that is – like the wobbling toddler.

Let Luke's accurate, ordered account of Jesus' birth guide you this Advent. I hope it helps you towards a faith that's increasingly stable and clear.

Heavenly Father, in the busiest month of the year, give us the settled stability that comes from seeing Jesus accurately, fully, clearly, and coherently. Reorder our muddled minds and capture our distracted hearts. Settle our lives on a vision of Jesus that is in keeping with his true glory. In his name. Amen.

Heaven may seem silent at times, but God is never inactive.

Throughout their long childless marriage, Zechariah and Elizabeth must have appealed repeatedly to the God they faithfully served. They experienced personally what the whole nation of Israel had known for 450 years: a silent heaven.

Four hundred and fifty years without a prophet speaking the word of God! *Was anything happening?* The faithful among the nation – like Zechariah and Elizabeth – went on hoping that God had the fulfilment of all his promises in hand. But it takes effort to pray when the answer is delayed…

It was while Zechariah, a senior priest, was praying for the people in the Temple of Jerusalem that God finally broke his silence. And the angelic message was worth the wait, because it confirmed that a longed-for promise was about to be fulfilled.

"Zechariah and Elizabeth, cancel your bowls club membership and prepare for parenthood! A son is on his way. Call him John. And the joy won't be yours alone: your son has a mission to the whole people, one they've been expecting for centuries!"

With his closing words, the last Old Testament prophet, Malachi, announced the coming of a figure just like the great Elijah (Malachi 4:5). He was to bring spiritual revival to the people, to prepare them for the coming of – look at verse 17! – *the Lord God himself.* The Lord God was on his way. John was to be the Elijah-like herald.

When heaven seems silent, *know that God is still active*. His promises may seem at times to disappear from view – like a river that suddenly plunges underground. For example, it may seem to us now that Jesus has forgotten to return. But the river of his purpose is still flowing, and it always re-emerges.

Zechariah and Elizabeth teach us that we mustn't stop praying, even if heaven does seem silent. Prayer places us at the centre of the action when the silence eventually breaks.

Father God, we praise you for your promises which can never fail. Help us to hold on to them when heaven seems silent. May we never give up believing that you will do more through our prayers than we can ask or imagine. Fulfil your purposes for us and through us. In Jesus' name. Amen.

What a crashing anti-climax! God's silence was broken. Zechariah ought to have danced around the temple for joy. Instead, an old enemy reared up: the sin of unbelief.

It is sobering because it was so out of character. Zechariah had kept God's law blamelessly for years, but in this defining moment he blew it. It's like the best fielder in the team dropping the catch that would have won the game.

Verse 18 records his suspicious question: "How can I be sure of this? I am an old man and my wife is well on in years." Had Zechariah forgotten that Israel's story was full of births to elderly and barren couples?

Mercifully, Gabriel struck him dumb, not dead. Still, his disobedience had significant consequences. The expectant crowd outside figured he'd seen a vision. But what was it? *Zechariah couldn't tell them.* Heaven had been silent for 450 years. Zechariah's unbelief extended the silence by nine months!

However, we also see clearly from his story that unbelief cannot ultimately stop the purpose of God. He works in spite of – and even through – Zechariah's faithless response.

Zechariah asked for certainty that Gabriel's message was true. He was given this certainty in an unexpected way: the moment he realised he couldn't talk, he had all the confirmation needed.

And God pressed on with John's miraculous conception, regardless of Zechariah's unbelief. That nine month frustration gave Zechariah opportunity to reflect deeply on what was happening. It made the song of praise he sang when John arrived all the more powerful (Luke 1:67-79).

"See to it, brothers and sisters, that none of you has a sinful, unbelieving heart that turns away from the living God" (Hebrews 3:12). That is a sobering warning from a God we have every reason to trust. We must take it to heart.

Zechariah's uncharacteristic reluctance to accept God's word should not surprise us. We can all relate to such wavering. We may often echo the words of the man who appealed to Jesus, crying out "I do believe; help me overcome my unbelief!" (Mark 9:24) Ask God to strengthen your faith and make you willing to trust him.

Heavenly Father, we believe, but help our unbelief. Let us never distrust your promises of salvation, provision, guidance, presence and victory. Let us never be over-awed when circumstances intimidate us. Fill us with the Holy Spirit today that by faith we may glorify you, being fully persuaded that you have power to do what you have promised. In Jesus' name. Amen.

God dispatches Gabriel again. He made his last announcement to a respected priest in the capital city. Now he must visit a peasant girl in an obscure village. At face value it is a lesser mission. In truth, it's far more important. We'll spend three days on it, focusing on Mary today, on her baby tomorrow, and on God the following day.

Three times the angel speaks to Mary, and three times Luke records her response. Her reactions develop from confusion, via a famous question, to submission.

The angel greets her as "highly favoured" (verse 28). She "was greatly troubled at his words and wondered what kind of greeting this might be" (verse 29). She's not so much terrified of the angel as baffled at how this exalted greeting could possibly apply to her. Perhaps Gabriel had the wrong person!

Mary's confusion springs from an unassuming humility, a self-effacing bewilderment that God should want to use her.

Gabriel then announces that Mary will bear the Messiah – the divine King promised throughout the Old Testament. Mary realizes that the promise presents a biological impossibility. Hence her famous question: "How will this be, since I am a virgin?" (verse 34).

Zechariah asked a question that *sounded* similar (verse 18), but his was loaded with unbelief. Mary's question springs from faith. She has no doubt that God will do what he has promised; she just can't see how.

Gabriel's answer leaves much unexplained. He only says enough to make it overwhelmingly clear that God will accomplish everything.

The initiative is God's. The power is God's. God's Spirit will overcome the human impossibilities. Mary is reassured with this all-sufficient explanation: "No word from God will ever fail" (verse 37).

Bear in mind that this plan will cost Mary. It risks her reputation and her marriage. But, confident in God's power and goodness, she places herself fully at his disposal: "May your word to me be fulfilled" (verse 38).

Mary is an outstanding example. Her unassuming humility stands in contrast to the entitlement we may sometimes feel. Her faith encourages us to pursue God's plans for his Kingdom even if we can't see how they are possible. Her submission inspires us to place our lives fully at his disposal, whatever the cost.

God our Father, make us like Mary. Forgive our sense of entitlement, and give us instead wonder and excitement that you want to use us for your glory. May the Holy Spirit's power overcome the impossible and accomplish your purposes through us. In the name of your Son, Jesus Christ, our Lord. Amen.

The first thing Gabriel says about Mary's son is that he must be called Jesus. It means, "The LORD is Salvation". Who is this Saviour, and from what does he save? Three contrasts between Jesus and John the Baptist make it clear:

1) John had a human mother and father, but Jesus was the son of a virgin

Not since God made Adam had he produced a human being by such a direct intervention of his creative power. This tells us that Jesus was a new start for the human race.

We certainly needed a new start. From the moment our race fell into sin and death, a new beginning was promised. The offspring of a woman (Genesis 3:15) would destroy the devil's work. Note, the offspring of a woman, with no mention of a man. Jesus' virgin conception identifies him as the promised human conqueror.

2) John is great in the sight of God, but Jesus is the great Son of God

John was born to become "great in the sight of the Lord" (1:15). Jesus' greatness is greater. Verse 32: "He will be great, and will be called the Son of the Most High." John was a mighty servant of God, but Jesus is God's unique Son. Jesus shared God's nature; John only preached about it.

How could Mary's son share God's Divine nature? In verse 35 Gabriel's delicate explanation points to the mysterious work of God's Spirit within her. Jesus would be fully the son of Mary, because of her biological involvement in his conception – so he would share Mary's human nature. And he would be Son of God because of God's spiritual involvement in his conception – so he would share God's divine nature.

3) John was a provisional prophet, but Jesus is the eternal King

John's ministry was time-limited, lasting only until the Lord had come. Jesus' Kingdom will never end. He was born to inherit the throne of Israel's greatest king, David, to fulfil God's promise that one of David's descendants would rule forever (verse 33).

An eternal reign? If a king is to rule forever, he must outlast all rivals. He must resist the corruption that has sunk many civilisations. And he must overcome death. King Jesus will do all that.

Who is the Saviour, and what does he save us from? He is the Son of God, born as man. He comes to destroy the devil, to atone for sin and to conquer death. He establishes a Kingdom of eternal peace, and he invites us all to enter.

God chose the name Jesus because he wants our first thought of his Son to be "Saviour!" Don't let this moment pass without using that name to address and praise this glorious Son, this eternal King, this supreme Saviour.

All praise to you great Saviour, glorious Son of God and conquering son of Mary. We gladly submit ourselves to your everlasting rule. May the Spirit who overshadowed Mary assure our hearts that sin and death, the devil and judgement no longer rule over us. Through your saving love. Amen.

Luke makes three direct references to God in his account of Gabriel's visit to Mary. They highlight three uplifting truths about our Father in heaven.

1) God chooses his means

"In the sixth month of Elizabeth's pregnancy, God sent the angel Gabriel..." (verse 26). Notice how carefully this event has been planned. He chose which angel to send – Gabriel. He chose the timing – in the sixth month of Elizabeth's pregnancy. He chose the woman – Mary.

The mention of King David's name in relation to Joseph, Mary's fiancé, tells us that God had been choosing his means long before this conversation took place. David's family had been chosen to bring the Messiah into the world. God was about to act on that one-thousand-year-old choice.

His plan doesn't make us impersonal pieces on his board. We come alive, as Mary did, when we offer ourselves to serve his purposes.

2) God secures his ends

"God will give him the throne of his father David ...his kingdom will never end" (verses 32-33).

Over the years many groups have attempted to shape the world's future. They may succeed for a while, creating chaos in the attempt. In the end they collapse. Their downfall has many causes, but the ultimate reason no human project can lay hold of the future is that God has handed it to his Son.

From the moment Jesus was conceived, that microscopic Person became the world's future. His divine presence in the human race set history on an unswerving course to a future no one can thwart.

3) God does it all by his unstoppable grace

"No word from God will ever fail" (verse 37).

Parents know what it's like to make promises to their children that they are unable to fulfil. "Yes, I'll fix it for you" we say, only to find the repair job is too difficult or time runs out. God the Father never over-promises, because his power is limitless.

A virgin to conceive in order to provide a sinless Saviour for sinners? No problem! A resurrection from the dead to ensure that this human being will reign forever? The Holy Spirit's got it covered!

We cannot tell how God will do all he has promised: win the nations, raise the dead and recreate the heavens and earth. But this we know, and take encouragement from today: nothing is impossible for him.

Father God, all glory to you. We praise you for your plan, initiated and accomplished by your own power. We believe that you have prepared good works for us to do today. Give us, your vulnerable and weak servants, the willingness and strength to do them. We pray in dependence on the Spirit and in anticipation of Jesus' eternal rule. Amen.

Mary must have been in a state of some turmoil as Gabriel left her. What would Joseph say? And her family? Mary lost no time in following up the sign the angel had given (verse 36). If Elizabeth was miraculously six months pregnant, then she could understand Mary's situation better than anyone.

This extraordinary meeting between the two expectant mothers confirmed the faith of both. Mary must have been rehearsing an explanation of her pregnancy as she travelled, but she didn't need to give it. The moment Elizabeth heard Mary's greeting, she prophesied: "Blessed are you among women, and blessed is the child you will bear!" (verse 42).

How did Elizabeth even know that Mary was pregnant? She couldn't phone ahead to explain. And Mary would not have been showing as she walked towards her cousin's house. No – the Holy Spirit told Elizabeth beforehand as a way of confirming Mary's faith.

How did the Spirit tell her? Remember what John was destined to do: he was to announce the Lord's coming. He was eager to get to work! Even from the womb the mighty prophet within Elizabeth testified to the Almighty Lord within Mary.

He did this by leaping in Elizabeth's womb the moment Mary entered the house. By the Spirit's inspiration, that leap revealed to Elizabeth the true identity of Mary's child: "why am I so favoured, that the mother of my Lord should come to me?" (verse 43).

This encounter must have strengthened the faith of Mary and Elizabeth. It strengthens our own faith as we read about how God kept and confirmed his promises to these two inspirational women.

There is good reason to focus on faith at this point in Luke's narrative. Faith is the essential response to God, his word and his purposes. Elizabeth declares it in verse 45: "Blessed is she who has believed that the Lord would fulfil his promises to her!"

We may not be entitled to expect God to confirm and sustain our faith through such dramatic signs as we read about here. Yet he does still strengthen our faith through the fellowship of likeminded believers. If you are discouraged in the Christian life, it might be because you are lacking this sort of fellowship. Seek it! And if you have this fellowship, thank God who gives it as a gift, and treasure it.

Father God, we thank you for confirming Mary's faith in a way that confirms and inspires ours too. When we are in turmoil, strengthen our trust in you. Fill us with the same Holy Spirit who gave Elizabeth her clear and joyful knowledge of Jesus, and lead us to likeminded sisters and brothers so we can encourage each other. In the name of the Lord Jesus Christ. Amen.

Mary's visit to Elizabeth lifted her faith, and prompted the song often known by its first word in Latin: *Magnificat*. "My soul *magnifies* the Lord..."

We'll spend three days on the song, focusing today on what Mary's soul did: it magnified the Lord. It's not that she made God bigger; she made him appear greater in her perspective.

My Grandad always read his newspaper through a magnifying glass. His paper didn't grow, it only seemed enlarged.

Our souls – our minds, hearts, spirits or inner selves – are always magnifying something. And in this situation, Mary's soul could easily have magnified the wrong things:

On the one hand, she could have magnified her privileges. She had been chosen for the highest honour in human history. Surely she wasn't above the temptation of pride.

What is pride, but a turning of our soul's magnifying glass onto its own privileges, abilities and achievements? Anyone familiar with their own soul will understand the potential danger Mary faced.

Alternatively, she could have magnified her problems. Divorce and disgrace were real possibilities. We could understand if, on hearing Elizabeth's confirmation, she had broken down in tears of despair: "So it really is happening! Oh no! What a mess!"

Fear and self-pity magnify our problems and shrink God in our perspective. The molehills become mountains, and obscure the eternal Rock of our salvation. But when we fix him in our sights, problems and privileges fade.

It often takes exertion to awaken our inner lives out of their habitual drowsiness to magnify God. It requires still more energy when we are drunk on privileges or burdened by problems. But make it your daily duty and joy to magnify him. Then the whole world will appear in the right perspective, as it did to Mary in this inspired song.

Heavenly Father, we magnify you. Eternal Son and Saviour, Jesus Christ, we magnify you. Holy Spirit, we magnify you. Forgive our self-centredness which so often leads us to magnify our privileges or problems. Our souls magnify you today, Father, Son and Holy Spirit. Amen.

Mary's soul magnified the Lord. Why? Verse 48 begins with the explaining word "for", alerting us that she's about to give her reason. Two reasons, in fact:

The first reason is personal: the Lord God had treated her with the kindest regard.

"Regards" is a common way to sign off a polite email. When you get a message ending "With kind regards", you can feel the warmth. God had treated Mary with the kindest regard, a kindness infinitely greater than she felt her lowly status deserved: "He has been mindful of the humble state of his servant" (verse 48).

Mary was of little account in social terms. Didn't King Herod or the High Priest have a suitable daughter? If so, they were ignored as the Lord regarded Mary.

But her humility is not just about social status. It's a question of Mary's self-understanding: she considers herself lowly, aware that she doesn't deserve God's attention. I suggest that she would have been stunned at the treatment she had received no matter where she stood on the social ladder.

The second reason she magnifies the Lord is that the Lord God had invested her with eternal significance: "From now on all generations will call me blessed" (verse 48).

Very few names outlive their own generation, let alone their civilisation. Surely only a deranged megalomaniac would claim that their name will be celebrated until the end of the world! Mary's will. But she is the opposite of a megalomaniac. She knows it's only in connection with Jesus that her name will live throughout history.

Why did Mary's soul magnify the Lord? Because he first magnified her. The difference is that he should be magnified. She had no reason to expect any such honour. God gave her these privileges out of sheer love, grace and kindness.

Mary was blessed to a unique degree. But it is only a matter of degree. All believers have been treated with God's kindest personal regard. All of us are invited to offer our lives to serve a Kingdom that will last forever.

Almighty Father, we stand amazed in the presence of Jesus, and wonder how you have loved and regarded us. Put Mary's sense of amazement into our hearts. Use us today for your purposes that we, like her, might contribute to the Kingdom that will last throughout all generations. In the name of Jesus and in the power of the Spirit. Amen.

Mary knew that her son would reign for ever. What will his eternal reign be like? How will this eternal reign confront the history of the world that is hurtling towards it? We will find out in this third reflection on her song.

A great principle straddles history and eternity. It applies now and forever. Verse 50: "His mercy extends to those who fear him from generation to generation."

The world will be sifted by this principle: there is mercy for all who humble themselves before God and his King, Jesus. It's certain. It is also certain that those who refuse to humble themselves enough to fear him will fall.

Mary can see exactly what this means in practice: a great reversal is coming.

Throughout history the rich and powerful have been on top. In the end they will be cast down, while those who fear God's King will be raised up (verses 51-52). Many of those exalted will prove to have been among the poorest in this age, with nothing to depend on except the promise of God (verse 53).

The reversal hasn't happened yet, but Mary speaks of it in the past tense to emphasise that it is certain. How could she be so sure?

God's promise-keeping faithfulness in the past confirms his promise-making trustworthiness for the future (verses 54-55). Just look how he dealt with Israel and kept his promises to Abraham: God promised Abraham a land, and he delivered. The nation of Israel was born, as promised. A Saviour was promised, one unique descendant of Abraham to bless all nations and reign forever. Now the promised child was growing in Mary's womb!

On the strength of God's proven faithfulness, Mary knew the great reversal was coming. History is still heading towards it.

We need to learn to live as though the reversal has already been fully accomplished, even if that puts us out of sync with our age. Take a lesson from long-haul air travel. To reduce jet lag, you set your watch on departure to the time at your destination. It prepares your body for the new time zone. You sleep and wake by the hands of your watch, not by the feeling in your eyelids.

The time to adjust to the great reversal is now, before it is finally enforced. Seek God's mercy now. Leave the proud behind, and set your watch to the time zone of Christ's everlasting Kingdom.

Father God, we magnify your Son, Jesus Christ, the eternal King. Let your mercy extend to us today as we stand in fear of you. Send Jesus soon, to lift up his people and to scatter the proud. Fill us with spiritual insight so our hearts are not captivated by the pomp and show of this world, but remain fixed on the coming reversal. For Jesus' glory. Amen.

Everyone knew it was a miracle. This birth to a very elderly woman would have been a sensation. Today it would make front page headlines in tabloid newspapers. All Elizabeth's friends recognised that God had shown her miraculous mercy (verse 57).

They must also have known that the miracle child was destined for something special. His conception came in the wake of a vision so powerful that it had left Zechariah dumb. The fact he was unable to explain what was happening would only have increased the nervous excitement. It crackled in the air at the naming ceremony.

The occasion didn't go as expected. At the critical moment in the ceremony a tension flared up between God's purpose and the enthusiastic public.

This tension was over the baby's name. The gathered friends and neighbours knew the tradition. Sons took their names from their fathers. "He's going to be called Zechariah," they decided, practically writing the name in indelible ink in the registrar's record.

Elizabeth's objection is emphatic. Literally she says, "No! But he shall be called John" (verse 60).

Perhaps Zechariah would show more respect for the traditions than his wife. They consult him with hand signals. (It seems he had been struck deaf as well as dumb.) Zechariah writes his verdict: "His name is John" (verse 63).

The name "John" means "The LORD is gracious". And what happens next is a powerful illustration of God's grace. Zechariah had been under judgement, but it is removed before everyone's eyes. His speech returns and he bursts out in praise.

This ramps up the sense of anticipation even higher. What would this child become (verse 66)?

Let's leave them rejoicing as we take a sober moment to emphasise that tension over the name. Human beings have their ways, their traditions and their expectations. Woe betide anyone who defies them!

Later, Jesus will defy human expectations. He will fall foul of the public's inflexibility, and it will contribute to his death.

Our cultural traditions can easily be mistaken for spiritual truths. It takes humble self-awareness to see where we are guilty of that fatal confusion ourselves. There's great virtue in an uncomplaining willingness to renounce such traditions when it serves the growth of God's Kingdom.

Father God, thank you for your clear intention to show us grace in Jesus Christ. Give us wisdom to distinguish the ways of his Kingdom from our cultural values, so that we may be flexible and willing to move forward with you. Fill us with your joy today, and with discernment from the Holy Spirit. In Jesus' name. Amen.

Zechariah's joy had been like fizzy champagne in a corked bottle. Anticipation bubbled within him during those silent months. Now the joy explodes in a song of pent-up praise.

Today we'll take the first part of the song (verses 68-75), which looks back to the promises Jesus fulfils; tomorrow, the second half (verses 76-79), which looks ahead to the future he will bring.

As Zechariah looks back, two Old Testament figures fill his mind, along with one Old Testament event.

One figure is David. God promised Israel's greatest king that the universe's eternal King would be raised up from his family line (2 Samuel 7:16). It took 1000 years. But in Jesus, the adopted son of Joseph – a descendant of David – God had raised up "a horn [a king, that is] of salvation for us in the house of his servant David" (verse 69).

The other figure is Abraham. God swore an oath to him, establishing an unconditional covenant that through his offspring all nations would be blessed (Genesis 12:1-3). One unique descendant was in mind, one particular son of Abraham with the power to secure such a great outcome: 1800 years later, that descendant was about to be born.

Now for the Old Testament event that shapes Zechariah's imagery. It's the Exodus of Israel from Egypt.

The LORD visited his people in Egypt and rescued them so they might serve him. In Jesus he visits again, this time to stay (verse 68). This time the salvation is eternal.

And now he enables us to serve him without trembling. Israel worshipped in terror as the mountain shook (Exodus 19:18). But Jesus saves us to enable us to "serve him without fear in holiness and righteousness before him all our days" (verses 74-75).

Dwell on that thought today. God saves us for a purpose: that we serve him *without fear*.

There is no need to look anxiously over our shoulders as we work for him. We don't need to hold back in his service for fear of failure. He is not looking to lash us with criticism. Quite the opposite. We do him great honour when we serve him brimming with the same joy that exploded from Zechariah's lips like a cork flies from a bottle.

Father in heaven, we praise you for binding yourself to Abraham in a covenant you have kept. We thank you for committing yourself to enthrone David's descendant forever. We worship you, Jesus, Son of David, for the freedom you have won for us. Make us your fearless, righteous and holy servants today. In the power of the Spirit. Amen.

Jesus' birth brought the past to its appointed climax and set the future's course. The first part of Zechariah's song reviewed the fulfilled past. The second prophesies the promised future. We will consider those prophecies today.

First, Zechariah speaks about his own son John. Then he looks ahead to Jesus, describing him as "the rising sun" (verse 78).

If Jesus is pictured as the morning sunrise, John can be described as the pre-dawn prophet. His role will be to awaken slumbering Israel, going before the Lord "to prepare the way for him, to give his people the knowledge of salvation through the forgiveness of their sins" (verses 76-77).

Suppose we only had the first part of Zechariah's song. We might think he was expecting John and Jesus to bring political salvation for Israel. The second half of his song suggests otherwise.

John isn't destined to train an army or gather a political movement. He will prepare Israel to receive the forgiveness of their sins, exposing their broken relationship with God which only Jesus can mend.

John is the pre-dawn prophet. Immediately after him comes Jesus, the radiant dawn: "the rising sun will come to us from heaven to shine on those living in darkness and in the shadow of death, to guide our feet into the path of peace" (verses 78-79).

I've taken the poetic phrase "radiant dawn" from the first line of a piece of Advent music that I love. It's by the Scottish composer Sir James MacMillan and its text is one churches have traditionally sung on 21st December for over 1500 years. On the shortest day of the year – in the Northern Hemisphere, at least – we can declare the victory of eternal light!

Zechariah has also borrowed his phrase "the rising sun". It comes from the prophets Isaiah (60:1-2) and Malachi (4:2). They prophesied the dawning of an inextinguishable light. Jesus is that promised light. Darkness must give way before him. Sin will flee from the light of his forgiveness, and the shadow of death will vanish.

The victory is certain, but the image of the rising sun implies that its effect will be seen gradually. The cool pink light warms into a glowing orange. The radiant dawn blazes into full morning and a bright midday that never ends. In the same way Bethlehem's light will prevail gradually. At times it will seem extinguished, but eventually it will entirely banish the darkness.

Zechariah's song is carried on an overwhelming tide. It's the tide of God's mercy. None of the gifts he mentions is deserved: John, Jesus, salvation, light and forgiveness. It all flows freely out from "the tender mercy of our God" (verse 78).

Can we feel that current carrying us? Your December schedule might be at its busiest right now. Make mental space, even for a few minutes, and ask the Spirit who inspired Zechariah to fill you with wonder at God's mercy in Christ.

Gracious Spirit of God, we turn from the darkness of sin and ask that Jesus, the radiant dawn, might shine on us. May his presence give us light in our darkness and guide us safely into the path of peace. Dispel our fear, and set our lives ablaze with joyful praise for all the Father's mercies. In the name of Jesus, the light of the world. Amen.

Luke writes, "In those days Caesar Augustus issued a decree that a census should be taken of the entire Roman world..." These words begin the most famous narrative in history.

Today we'll explore three implications of Luke's precise historical references, paying special attention to Caesar Augustus, the Roman Emperor.

First, we learn that Jesus' birth was an event in history. It took place in the flow of universally-known events.

Remember that Luke was writing to inspire certainty in Theophilus, a new believer. Theophilus was a non-Jew. He might have read chapter 1 and wondered if the stories were perhaps just that – myths and legends of an alien culture. Luke insists that Jesus' birth was a real event at a precise time.

Second, we learn that God has a global vision.

In chapter 1, Luke's narrative takes place within a local Jewish world. With the mention of Caesar Augustus, the story's horizon suddenly expands to include the whole known world.

It's no coincidence that Luke – whose contribution to the Bible comes in two volumes – begins with this mention of the Roman Emperor. He ends with the Apostle Paul appealing to Caesar and preaching the gospel in Rome. The whole world is in God's view from the start.

Third, we learn that the Roman Emperor is only a servant of the true King, Jesus.

Augustus' census brought about a circumstance vital to the establishment of Jesus' Kingdom: that he was born in Bethlehem, the ancestral home of King David, where the Messiah was destined to be born.

Why did Caesar call his census? He probably wanted to increase his tax revenue. But God made Caesar's plan serve the interests of his ultimate King, Jesus.

In contrast to this greater King, we might be tempted to ask, "Caesar *who?*"

We should take encouragement from these three observations. We don't just have a good story, we have solid history. And Jesus' Kingdom is not an irrelevant subculture. That's how some portray it, and even believers can unwittingly shrink it to that level in their minds. No – Jesus' reign has the power of the sovereign God behind it, and the whole world in its sights.

Our Father, you have raised the Kingdom of Jesus above all worldly kingdoms. Send him soon, that his rule may be seen. Keep our faith anchored to the historic events of his life, death and resurrection; and lift our eyes to see him at work throughout the world today. May we live by the inspiration of the Holy Spirit, confident that Jesus is Lord. Amen.

Nativity plays manage to eke a lot of drama out of what Luke says in two simple verses:

"While they were there, the time came for the baby to be born, and she gave birth to her firstborn, a son. She wrapped him in cloths and placed him in a manger, because there was no guest room available for them" (verses 6-7).

There are so many details we don't know. They *might* have tried many inns. The manger *might* have been in a stable or possibly in a cave, a courtyard or on the street. All we can say for sure is that the manger wasn't in Mary's birth plan!

It must have prompted Mary and Joseph to ask the question: *can this be right?*

Gabriel said the child would be the Son of God, the King and Saviour of the world, yet here they were with the animals! Had the wheels come off the plan?

Jesus' disciples would later wrestle with exactly the same questions. The cross: can *this* be right? The apostles could have asked the same question as, one by one, they suffered for Jesus' Kingdom. When difficulties hit us, we also ask: "Can God possibly still be at work?"

But there is no mistake. Indeed, God often works most powerfully while we are too busy dealing with the crisis to notice.

The manger was exactly the way God wanted his Son to make his decisive entrance into the world. It sent a clear message: he was born in a mess for messy people; born in poverty to overturn human pride; born as a helpless baby to prove God's weakness stronger than human strength; and born under a cloud of misunderstanding. He was a rejected outsider from the start, that his birth might foreshadow his death.

It was exactly right, even though it must have felt wrong. God was at work – not despite the fiasco, but through the fiasco itself.

Luke doesn't tell us how Mary and Joseph handled their tough situation. We only know how easily we become discouraged when our circumstances seem to contradict God's promised love. We must learn from the manger scene: it might be precisely in these troubling moments that Jesus is making his entrance.

Father God, you are for us not against us. Keep us strong in faith when circumstances seem to contradict the love you have promised. Forgive us for how easily we become discouraged. Give us the mind of the Holy Spirit that we might discern your wisdom and power in what would otherwise appear foolish and weak. In the name of Jesus. Amen.

Joy and song and light. This passage seems to ring and shine. We'll enjoy its glow over the next four days.

Today, the message of the first angel, who announced Jesus' birth: "Do not be afraid. I bring you good news that will cause great joy for all the people. Today in the town of David a Saviour has been born to you; he is the Messiah, the Lord" (verses 10-11).

Why is it such good news?

First, the Saviour is born. To save from what? Zechariah's song has already explained. He will save his people from sin through his own self-sacrifice. He will save them from the shadow of death through the light of his resurrection (1:77-79).

Jesus didn't come to tell us how to be saved, but to save us. The difference is crucial. He doesn't stand on the edge of the icy river and offer drowning humanity advice on how to escape. That's how the prophets and teachers of other belief systems, religious and secular, approach the human condition. Instead Jesus dives into the icy, dark water to lift us out of sin and death by his own death for our sin.

Second, Christ is born. Or Messiah. The first is the Greek and the second the Hebrew title for the eternal King, destined to be born as King David's descendant. The prophets painted his reign on the largest canvas imaginable: he will overturn death and rebuild the whole of creation.

At last the Messiah had arrived: "He's down there, shepherds, in Bethlehem, the city of David, and you are the first to know."

Third, the Lord is born. Who else could accomplish everything promised of this Saviour and King? No one less than Almighty God can deliver eternal salvation and never-ending rule.

As you process this wonderful message, consider two of the angel's words which are easy to miss. The Saviour is born *"to you"* (verse 11). For the shepherds, yes, but also for you. He is born for each of us, personally.

It's possible to agree that the message is true but find no joy in it. Joy is lit within us when we grasp that this Saviour, King and Lord is our own. He is yours. Believe it with fearless joy.

Jesus, we look to you for salvation, we submit to you as King and we worship you as Lord. By the power of the Holy Spirit convince our hearts that you were born for us, and let this assurance fill us with joy. Father, we thank you for Jesus. Amen.

Today, let's hear the song of the heavenly host – the army of angels that bursts out of heaven the moment the first angel tells the shepherds that the Lord God is wrapped in cloths and lying in a manger:

"Glory to God in the highest heaven, and on earth peace to those on whom his favour rests" (verse 14).

That phrase trips off the tongue as if its two halves naturally belong together. Really we ought to pause, astonished. By rights, God's glory and mankind's peace are opposed to one another.

God's shining glory is the dazzling outward display of his inner goodness, truth and righteousness. And yet when he shows his glory, we are exposed as the opposite of good, true and righteous.

If we were playing a game of "complete the sentence" and started with the words "Glory to God in the highest", we could fittingly add the words: "And doom to all people on earth!" No wonder the shepherds were terrified when the glory of God shone around them.

How, then, can the angels' sentence end with the words "and peace to those on whom his favour rests"?

Notice exactly what prompted the angel choir to sing: "a Saviour has been born to you...you will find a baby...lying in a manger". That's the key.

The Saviour in the manger is God's highest glory. What a gracious God, to be most glorified in freely laying aside his shining majesty out of sheer love!

And the Saviour in the manger is mankind's true peace. The angels are not referring primarily to peace among people, but peace between sinful human beings and God. Lying humbly in the manger was the decisive step towards the humiliation of the cross, where Jesus will make peace through his blood (Colossians 1:20).

This peace is offered to the whole world, but it's only possessed by "those on whom his favour rests". That is, people like Zechariah and Mary, and anyone who shares their faith in Jesus.

Jesus resolves and unites two principles that would otherwise remain in conflict: God's glory and mankind's peace. Because the Saviour lay in the manger that night, there is nothing to fear on earth and everything to hope for in heaven.

Sit still for a moment, and give God all the glory by consciously enjoying the peace he has established through Jesus.

Father God, you are glorified in making peace with us through your Son. Make us conscious of this peace today, that it may rule our hearts and govern our relationships. Give us the angels' insight and fill us with their joy. In the name of Jesus, the Lord in the manger. Amen.

On Christmas night the angel brought the shepherds good news. The shepherds told Mary and Joseph, along with the startled residents of Bethlehem. And so began a chain of communication that remains unbroken to this day.

The angel says to the shepherds: "I bring you good news" (verse 10). This phrase became the label used to describe Jesus' entire message: *the good news* or, as the phrase comes to us through Old English, *the gospel*.

Without the angel's explanation, the events in Bethlehem would make little sense. Suppose the shepherds had just stumbled upon a baby in a manger. What would they think? His situation would have inspired pity, not joy. But their hearts are filled with joy because the angelic description of Jesus' identity and mission is ringing in their ears.

The joy of the message makes them messengers: "They spread the word concerning what had been told them about this child" (verse 17). That's striking for two reasons:

First, the shepherds were gripped more by what they had heard than by what they had seen. Bear in mind that they saw sights no one else has ever witnessed. God's glory blazed in the sky above them while an angelic army sang his praise! When we see an amazing sight – like the Victoria Falls or the Grand Canyon – we want to describe to others what we saw. But the shepherds were most concerned to recount what the angel said about the child.

A second striking feature of the shepherd's announcement is that they don't direct people to the manger. The shepherds seemed to think it was enough for the residents of Bethlehem to know what the angel had said about Jesus. No visit was necessary, because the event lives in the hearts of those who hear and believe the good news.

Luke is showing us how we can have our share in the events, even though they happened so long ago. The angel's message never expires, and as we put our trust in it we can have as much joy 2000 years later as the shepherds knew on that first Christmas night.

God intends that we become part of the chain of communication the angel began. Someone must have told us the message. Who was it? Thank God for them. And if you believe this message of joy, who can you share it with today?

Father God, we praise you for the gospel – your own announcement about Jesus, your Son, our Saviour. Thank you that through this good news we have a share in the events of Jesus' life: his birth, death and resurrection. Give us joy as we believe the gospel, and fire us by your Spirit to pass it on today. In Jesus' name. Amen.

Here's some advice from the towering nineteenth century preacher C.H. Spurgeon: "Read the Bible carefully, then meditate, meditate, meditate." Mary would agree.

In chapter 2 Mary experiences an exaggerated version of what happens to all parents when their first child is born. Suddenly they recede. There are no photos of them anymore, as the focus shifts to the baby! Only one brief comment gives away Mary's response to events: "But Mary treasured up all these things and pondered them in her heart" (verse 19). What thoughts were in her mind?

She would have reflected on the nine months since Gabriel announced Jesus' arrival. The promise had been fulfilled. God's plan for this world had just taken the decisive step forward.

The previous hours had left Mary with much to contemplate. Childbirth gives any new mother plenty to think about. Mary's mind also had to process the accommodation fiasco and the midnight visit of the shepherds with their jubilant message.

As her mind chewed it all over, surely she must have looked ahead too. The future lay before Mary like a page covered with question marks. How would this baby who couldn't sit up at all sit one day on the universe's throne? What would the God-man be like as a toddler, child, teenager and adult? How was Mary to relate to her son who was also her Lord? Would he ever be truly hers, or must she share him with the world?

There were many imponderables, and the tensions remained unresolved for years. In the meantime, her soul treasured everything she did know for sure. The word of God was fixed: "his kingdom will never end... For no word from God will every fail" (1:33, 37).

God's word is treasure to our hearts, but we often receive it like money boxes that have lost the rubber stopper from the bottom. The treasure drops in, and immediately drops out. Fear and uncertainty soon rush in to fill up the empty space.

Mary's example teaches us to keep the treasure within us. Memorise God's word. Turn it over and over. Write it down. Enter it with a God-given imagination. Find musical settings and sing it. Just don't lose the treasure!

Father God, we are sorry that we often engage with your word superficially. Open our hearts to receive it, and give us the time and space to treasure it. Give us faith as we travel the unknown road towards the certain future you have promised in Jesus. In his name. Amen.

We seem to hit the earth with a bump as the excitement of Christmas night gives way to the legal ceremonies Jesus' parents performed for him. It may feel like going back to work in January after the excitement of Christmas celebrations. Luke mentions three ceremonies:

1. Jesus was circumcised and named when he was eight days old, receiving the sign of God's ancient covenant with Abraham.

2. Around five weeks later, the family took the ten-mile trip from Bethlehem to Jerusalem for Jesus – the firstborn in the family – to be presented to the Lord. Since the time of Moses, the Lord claimed ownership of the firstborn.

3. Finally, Jesus' mother had to offer the sacrifices for purification, because the blood associated with childbirth made her ceremonially unclean.

Why do we need to know these details? At least two reasons stand out:

First, it roots Jesus in a story that non-Jews have to learn as their own. Non-Jewish believers might imagine that God's purposes began at Jesus' birth. His participation in these long-established Jewish ceremonies prevents that misunderstanding. He was born into a plotline that runs right through the Old Testament.

It's vital to see Jesus in the context of Israel's story because otherwise he can be twisted into the shape of our own ideas. That's a sure way to lose the real Jesus. So believers from a non-Jewish background have no choice but to enter Old Testament history and own it.

Secondly, it declares Jesus' intention to stand in our place. We have to wonder why, as the Son of God, he was not exempt from ceremonies designed for sinners. Why did he have to be given to God as a firstborn son when he was already God's Son? He was taking our place. He was being treated like a sinful outsider because *that's what we are.*

These sacrifices in Jerusalem were just the start. He would keep God's law perfectly in our place. Eventually he would fully bear the judgement we sinful outsiders deserve, when he sacrificed himself for us on the cross.

If Jesus was to redeem us, whom the law condemns, he had to be born under the law himself (see Galatians 4:4-5). The Son had to be treated like a stranger, so that strangers can be treated like sons and daughters.

All glory to you, our Father, for this wonderful salvation. All glory to you, Lord Jesus, for submitting yourself to the law for law-breakers, and for making sinful outsiders the children of God. By the Spirit's power, make us as willingly obedient to the Father's purposes as you were. In your name. Amen.

There's a powerful book by the English Puritan Jeremiah Burroughs entitled *The Rare Jewel Of Christian Contentment.* Why is Christian contentment such a rare jewel when Jesus is more than the sum of all hopes?

We're going to spend three days in the contented company of the elderly pair Simeon and Anna. Let's hope their joy is catching!

Simeon's life was propelled forwards by hope. He shared the general hope preached by the prophets: God's King was coming to lift Jerusalem from the spiritual doldrums where it had languished for hundreds of years. In addition, the Spirit had told him specifically that he would see this King in his own lifetime.

Suddenly, the Spirit prompted him: "Today is the day, Simeon." Entering the temple, he not only saw the Lord's Messiah – he hugged him!

A song flowed out of him, known in church history by its first words in Latin: *Nunc Dimittis.* It combines two emotions we don't normally associate: perfect contentment and excited anticipation.

"Sovereign Lord, as you have promised, you may now dismiss your servant in peace. For my eyes have seen your salvation, which you have prepared in the sight of all nations: a light for revelation to the Gentiles and the glory of your people Israel" (verses 29-32).

There's contentment, because in Jesus the consolation Israel hoped for has come. Total salvation lies wrapped in his arms as he cradles the fulfilment of all true hope.

When Simeon says he's ready to die, it's the opposite of hopelessness. His hopes have been so entirely fulfilled that he's happy to surf this wave of joy straight into the heavenly life without delay.

Then there's anticipation. Jesus will be "a light to the Gentiles" – to the nations of the whole world.

Who said the elderly like sticking to the old ways? Not Simeon. As he bows out, he embraces the huge change that Jesus is destined to bring. Until that point, God's purposes had centred on Jerusalem. Soon they will extend to the whole earth. "Bring it on!" thinks Simeon.

Why is Christian contentment such a rare jewel when Jesus is the sum of all hopes? Perhaps it's because sometimes the "treasure" we hug closest to ourselves is not Jesus, but our own cherished possessions and dreams.

Father God, you gave Jesus to console your people, Israel, and to shine a light on all nations. Forgive our restless discontent. Shine in us today. By the Spirit's transforming work, may we find our lives' purpose not in pursuing what we hope to gain, but in Jesus. For your glory. Amen.

Today we will face Simeon's solemn prophecy. For the first time in Luke, here is an explicit statement of the turbulence Jesus will bring.

Are we willing to face this inevitable aspect of Christ's Kingdom? Instinctively, we're surprised when the truth of Jesus is disputed and despised, but we should expect turbulence for three reasons:

First, Jesus exposes hearts: "the thoughts of many hearts will be revealed" (verse 35). Jesus held a mirror to people's deepest motives. Later in Luke's gospel we see that opponents discovered this to their cost – they queued up to test him only to find themselves exposed (e.g. 10:25-37, 14:1-6, 20:1-8).

Jesus reveals hearts simply by virtue of who he is. He is God's Son. The way we treat an ambassador shows what we think of the ambassador's country. How much more does our treatment of Jesus reveal our true thoughts about his Father! Many hate Jesus for exposing their hearts.

Second, Jesus forces a decision. His presence creates a fork in Israel's road. It forces the question: either/or? For him, or against him? That remains the choice he presents. As a brand new follower of his recently said to me, "At last I've realised – there is no fence to sit on with Jesus!"

Third, Jesus determines destinies: "This child is destined to cause the falling and rising of many in Israel" (verse 34). With him around, there's no need to wait for the final judgement to know where a person will stand in relation to God. Our reaction to him now reveals his reaction to us on that Day.

There was turbulence ahead. Jesus would cut like a sword through Israel's religious hypocrisy and inflexible unbelief. Even Mary would feel the pain of it as her own misunderstandings were exposed and corrected (verse 35).

Simeon's prophecy doesn't directly predict that Jesus himself will suffer. However, it would have been hard for Mary not to draw this ominous implication. Her son's uncompromising ministry was bound to run into resentful opposition.

Exposing hearts, forcing decisions, determining destinies: Jesus still does all that, often through his followers. That means suffering may come to them too. Are we ready to follow him on these terms?

There are no others.

Father God, have mercy on us for our love of ease. Fill us instead with the Holy Spirit who filled your Son, Jesus Christ, and empowered him to lay down his life. Stand close to those suffering for their faith this Christmas. Make them aware of your presence, and assure them that you will lift them up. In the name of Jesus and for the good of all his loved ones. Amen.

Was Anna just very old, or staggeringly old? As you might pick up from the footnote in verse 37, the Greek text could be read in one of two ways, either making her 84 or around 104. We won't enter the debate. Instead, let's aim to be as energetic in sharing our faith as she was, however long we live.

Anna came up to Mary, Joseph and Jesus during Simeon's prophecy. As he finishes, we turn our attention to her.

There are many similarities between Anna and Simeon. Both are old. Both have lived lives of hopeful waiting, looking towards exactly the same event: the coming of God's Messiah to console and redeem Jerusalem.

Likewise, both are willing to accept the unsettling theme of Simeon's prophecy. Simeon utters it, and Anna – who arrived at that moment – joyfully accepts Jesus as Messiah regardless.

Yet there are important differences between Simeon and Anna too – differences that help to complete Luke's testimonies to the infant Jesus.

One obvious difference is that Simeon is a man and Anna a woman. In chapter 1, a woman and a man testified to Jesus: Mary and Zechariah. And it's the same in chapter 2 with Simeon and Anna. That's not a coincidence. Luke is building a complete and united testimony to Jesus. Men and women both testify. In addition, angels and humans praise his name. Uneducated shepherds and devout temple worshippers kneel before him.

Here's another difference between the two elderly believers. Simeon represents the end of an era as he expresses his readiness to die.

Meanwhile, perhaps unwittingly, Anna is a trailblazer for the new dawn. She tells all her friends about Jesus. She becomes an evangelist, declaring the good news in the heart of Jerusalem. Later, the apostles will follow her lead.

Anna's example is the antidote to a poison that is deadly to the life of God's Kingdom: weary cynicism. Long periods of waiting are a common cause of this progressively debilitating spiritual disease. "Is anything ever going to happen?" we ask in exasperation.

Simeon and Anna show us what treasures lie in store for us if we wait for God's purposes in an attitude of hope. Simeon's faithful waiting bore the fruit of total contentment. Anna's faithful waiting bore the fruit of evangelistic energy deep into her old age.

We may wait for Jesus' second coming our entire lives, departing before seeing his Kingdom arrive in full. No matter. Keep hope alive and expectation joyful. Know for sure that any emptiness we experience in the waiting time is only preparing us to receive more of his love in the end.

Father God, forgive our shallowness and cynicism, our discouragement and impatience. We thank you for Simeon's and Anna's combined testimony to Jesus. Give us the same contentment in him as they knew, and the same love, endurance and peace. Give us Anna's energy to share the gospel throughout our lives. In Jesus' name. Amen.

There are certain incidents in our children's lives that seem to reveal who the unique child really is: the time she stood up to that bully to protect her friend, or the care he took over building that new Lego set. As life goes on we realise that these apparently small incidents captured the essence of the adult the child was to become.

Luke only records one incident from Jesus' childhood, but it's enough. Jesus chose to disappoint his parents. He remained behind in Jerusalem after Passover and astonished the teachers in the temple with his wisdom. When challenged for his disobedience he declared that he was in his Father's house. This tells us all we need to know.

We've reached the climax of Luke's first two chapters. Everyone else has spoken about Jesus. *Now he speaks for himself:*

"Why were you searching for me? Didn't you know I had to be in my Father's house?" (verse 49). These questions refer back to two key themes from his infancy:

First, Jesus knew he was the Son of God. The angel told Mary that he would be called the Son of the Most High and the Son of God (1:32, 35). Jesus was growing in body and mind as the son of Mary. He was a human child – although with a unique aptitude for Bible study! But he already knew that he had an *additional* identity as the Son of God.

That leads to a second theme this incident refers back to: Jesus defies human assumptions. He'd done it from the start when his lowly birth challenged human expectations about God.

It turns out that his commitment to his Father will defy even his mother's expectations. It must have been hard for her to swallow: two days of anxious searching for the child who had never disobeyed before, and she got a telling off not an apology! Didn't she realise what his higher identity meant for him?

All Jesus' followers have to get used to their expectations of him being defied. His commitment to the Father led him to embrace the cross, against his disciples' expectations and advice. He could have confronted their exasperation with the same question he asked at twelve years old: "Didn't you know I had to attend to the things of my Father?"

As a follower of Jesus, never hug your own expectations too tightly – even on Christmas Eve, the day of great expectations. The Son of God reserves the right to defy our expectations. That's a good thing, though, because he will reshape them to serve his higher purpose.

Father, we praise and thank you that your Son was always totally committed to your purposes. Help us to hold our own expectations in life loosely, that we may have the humility to follow him all the way to the cross if necessary. Place your Kingdom at the top of our list of priorities at this expectant moment of the year. In the Spirit's power and the name of Jesus. Amen.

If you are reading this on 25th December – Happy Christmas!

The angel said to the shepherds, *"Today* in the town of David a Saviour has been born to you... "* (verse 11, emphasis added).

We don't know what date he was born. The church has settled on this day as the moment to remind itself that there really was a day.

On an actual day in history, during Augustus' census, Jesus was born. This is not a myth designed to illustrate a religious idea. God's own Son entered our history on a particular day to change its course forever:

- The Lord has come, joining himself to the lost human race forever.

- The King has come. Through his death and resurrection, he has gained the eternal throne of David. Every proud power will fall before him.

- The Saviour has come, to forgive sin, and to shine his light on those who live in darkness and the shadow of death.

The fulfilment of all God's promises was wrapped in cloths and lying in the manger on that actual day. In the words of an English cliché: "God's only gone and done it!"

The result of that "today" is a song of joy that still goes on. Jesus is the radiant dawn whose day never ends.

Five-hundred years ago, Martin Luther was searching for some adequate way to describe the joy we would feel if we truly grasped what that day meant. The best he could come up with was to suggest that if we fully understood it, our bodies would literally explode!

So take Jesus again today as the Lord you worship; and the King you obey; and the Saviour you trust. And know with a settled, joyful certainty that the peace of the eternal God is on you.

All glory to you, Father, for the gracious gift of Jesus your Son. All glory to you, Jesus: Saviour, King and Lord. All glory to you, Holy Spirit, for making his coming possible. May the radiant dawn blaze ever brighter until we see the full light of Jesus' never ending day. Lighten our darkness, shining in us and through us to the honour and glory of the name we love, Jesus Christ, our Lord. Amen.

Acknowledgements

My friend and editor Edmund Barns has enhanced *The Radiant Dawn* immeasurably. His literary craftsmanship is an inspiration to me, and an education. Thank you.

It was Katie, my wife, who first encouraged me to make these notes widely available. They were disseminated through friends and personal contacts in Advent 2018. I am grateful to those who received them warmly and encouraged me. Lois Ferguson and Jonathan Pountney at 10Publishing were among them. I thank the whole 10Publishing team for taking them on, bringing them to publication and getting them into your hands.

10 Publishing

a division of 10 of those.com

10Publishing is the publishing house of **10ofThose**. It is committed to producing quality Christian resources that are biblical and accessible.

www.10ofthose.com is our online retail arm selling thousands of quality books at discounted prices.

For information contact: **info@10ofthose.com**
or check out our website: **www.10ofthose.com**